Table of Contents

Introduction

Have you been thinking about getting a cute little puppy? I guess you probably have so many questions about this that you don't know which one to begin with. It is reasonable that you feel this way. The decision to bring a puppy home is not something that you can decide in a minute or two. There are so many things to consider when making such a huge step. You will first need to decide on the right breed for you. Then, you will need to do a small investigation and find a reputable breeder. And then when you finally bring this little ball of fur home, you will probably find yourself completely lost as you don't know what exactly to do now.

Don't worry. This book will be your guide from the very beginning of your puppy adventure. Besides some tips on choosing the right breed and the breeder, you will also learn how to prepare for this new member of your family, how to feed him, train and socialize him, how and what to play with him, as well as how to groom and take a good care of your puppy. So, as you can see, this book is the ultimate guide you can rely on from the very first day of your life with this new member of your family.

I would like to thank you for downloading this book and I hope you will enjoy reading! Please help to post a review on Amazon after reading, even if it is just a sentence or two. Your review will help me to improve further and provide greater contents to readers. If I have done well, let me know too as your encouragement will go a long way to motivate me to write more!

Chapter 1: How to Choose the Right Breed

Once you've decided to have a dog, you will need to choose the right breed for you and your family. There are more than 160 breeds and all of these are characterized by their own appearance, temperament, energy level, etc. So, deciding on the right breed for you requires doing a serious research.

When deciding on the breed, you need to look at the descriptions of breeds you are interested in and specifically look at the grooming and exercise requirements, trainability, and temperament of each breed. If possible, you can try to spend some time with the breeds you are interested in. For instance, you can go to a local breeder and ask him to let you spend some time with the dogs there. When you get some vague idea about a few breeds you are interested in, you can then search a bit more about these.

It's not only that the dog should be right for your family but your family should also be right for the dog. Thus, choosing the right dog depends on several factors, such as your lifestyle, a dog's temperament, your budget, etc. In that sense, it is wise to consider the following factors:

- **Lifestyle and living situations**

Choose a dog that is compatible with your lifestyle. For instance, although all dogs enjoy physical activity, there are certain breeds, such as Dalmatians, who need more than an hour of active exercise and play every day. If, for example, you can't follow this rhythm and like to stay indoors, then you should find a dog with a temperament similar to yours.

You also need to think about your living environment and choose a dog accordingly. For instance, if you have your own house with lots of space where your dog can run and play, then you can consider choosing some larger breeds like German shepherds, Labrador retrievers, etc. On the other hand, if you live in a small space and don't have some park nearby where you can let your dog run, then you should think of choosing smaller breeds, such as beagle or Welsh corgi because these don't mind if they are kept indoors. Think about the climate you live in as well simply because some breeds like bulldogs and pugs like colder weather more.

As dogs may trigger allergies, this is another thing to think about. In case you or some member(s) of your family have allergies, then it would be better to opt for breeds like the Portuguese water dog, the Maltese and Shih Tzu, because they are easier to manage.

- **Temperament**

The temperament of your new dog is important because since you have decided to get a dog in the first place, you certainly plan to have this dog around for years. So, you should make sure that you can live with this dog and that the dog's temperament is similar to yours. Bear in mind that while purebred dogs typically have the same treats as the other dogs of the same breed, mixed breeds normally exhibit the traits of both breeds. In that sense, ask yourself what kind of dog you want – a dog that doesn't mind staying indoors, an active dog, a dog friendly to strangers or a guard dog.

- **Size**

Think about the size as well. Although it may seem that smaller breeds don't need much space, it's actually not always the case, as some small dogs are very active and like to run around.

- **Grooming needs**

When you think about getting a dog, you should not forget that all dogs need proper care and grooming if you want them to stay healthy. However, some breeds require more care than others. If you don't have enough time to devote to grooming your dog, then you should definitely avoid those breeds which have long and curly coats, because you will need to groom these breeds several times per week. Also, bear in mind that some dogs may need professional grooming as well.

- **Health**

Also, inform yourself about some possible health issues, such as eye or hip problems, which a specific breed may be prone to. While still at a breeder, puppies can be screened for certain hereditary conditions, and this certification should be available to you when you go to look for a puppy.

- **Male or female**

Generally speaking, there are no significant differences between males and females. In case you want to keep a puppy as a pet, you will probably want your dog neutered or spayed, which in turn neutralized those subtle differences between the genders. On the other hand, if you want a dog to breed or show him, then you will need to take care of your intact male and female and prevent any unwanted breeding.

- **Trainability**

There are breeds for hunting, working, sporting, herding breeds, and these are all high-energy breeds, which means that they are trained to spend much time outside and that they have lots of energy, so that they can run all day long. If you want a quiet dog that will mostly spend time indoors, then don't choose these breeds.

If you want to get a dog for your kids, then you should consider breeds which are highly trainable. These breeds typically don't attach themselves to only one person but are very eager to spend time with children and they are usually family-oriented. Some popular and highly trainable breeds are German shepherds, Labrador retrievers, collies, and golden retrievers. In any case, if you have children, don't worry, as all breeds are great with children if socialized properly. There's one thing that may be helpful. It's usually better to choose larger breeds if you have small children. The reason behind this is simple. Small kids sometimes pull dog's ears or step on their feet and if a dog is small, it will be injured and bite your kid. On the other hand, larger breeds are sturdier and thus a better option for smaller kids.

- **Affordability**

Purchasing a dog is not the only thing you will need to pay for. You will have to think about all the money you will spend on your dog each month. So, here are some guidelines in terms of cost and which can help you when you choose the right breed for you. Smaller breeds are generally less expensive than larger breeds, because they eat less and their healthcare costs are less expensive. If you think of getting yourself a purebred dog, you should know that you will spend more money up front. Not only that! These purebred dogs are also prone to certain health problems, which is not a case with mixed breeds.

Start Your Search

So, make a checklist of characteristics you want your dog to have. Be honest to yourself about how much time you can spend with the dog. Dogs need both mental and physical exercise and if they don't get it, they are unhappy and when dogs are unhappy they become destructive.

Chapter 2: How to Choose the Right Breeder

The best place where you can get a puppy is a reputable breeder. If you still don't have any particular breeder in mind, you can find lists of breeders on the Internet, in magazines, ads, or you can ask your friends, local veterinary clinics, etc. One of the advantages of getting a puppy from a reputable breeder is that you also have someone whom you can turn to in case you have any problems with your puppy. Also, when you decide to buy a puppy from a breeder, it actually means that you will get a purebred, i.e. a dog of a specific breed.

As you have different dog breeds, there are different dog breeders as well. There are breeders who are truly enthusiastic and ethical about their work. They don't care about the money earned but about producing puppies with the highest behavior, ability and physical attributes of their breed. All those reputable breeders always strive to breed dogs with good genetic traits. On the other hand, there are breeders who don't care much about the puppies they produce but are concerned with breeding as many puppies as they can, so that they can later on sell them. If you want a puppy for your home, you want to avoid this kind of breeders.

A reputable breeder:

- follows recommended breeding guidelines.

- tests puppies for eye and hip conditions and informs owners of the results of these screening tests.

- allows you to see a puppy with its mother, so that you can see how the puppy is likely to turn out. You should be allowed to see the puppy with the rest of the litter as well.

- is willing to give answers to all your questions.

- gives you guidelines on how to raise your puppy properly, including the information on training and socializing.

- ensures you that they will be there any time you need help with your puppy.

- allows you to see all the puppies and handle them instead of offering you a specific one.

If you find out that some of your potential breeders don't follow these guidelines or you see that their puppies don't look happy, then you should look for a puppy at some other place.

In order to check if a breeder is reputable or not, you can always do a research to decide on their reputation. For instance, when you go to a breeder, you can ask some questions and make sure that:

- they can give you a copy of the Code of Ethics you can then review.

- they belong to any breed organizations or clubs.

- they require certain criteria of their breeding stock.

- they are aware of any health problems of the breed in question.

- they do any health testing for those problems.

- they have test results of both parents, which they are willing to give you to review.

- they tell you which vaccinations your puppy has already had and which ones it will still need to have.

- they socialize their puppies.

- they will give you some instructions on how to raise your puppy.

- they guarantee that they will take the puppy or dog back in case of any problem.

- they have certain requirements that a buyer must meet to get a puppy.

Depending on the answers you get, you will be able to decide if the person is a responsible breeder or not. So, as you can see, in order to choose the right and reputable breeder, you need to do a lot of research and ask lots of questions before you make any decision.

Chapter 3: Profiles of Some Popular Breeds

Golden Retriever

Golden retrievers adapt well to staying indoors. They are quiet and low-energy dogs that are easy to train, as they are eager to please their owners. These are friendly, tolerant, highly intelligent and loyal dogs. Golden retrievers are highly sociable and are known for their patience with children and for their kind and warm nature. Your Golden will require an hour of daily exercise and all sorts of activities, both mental and physical. When it comes to grooming, they shed particularly in the spring and fall, so you will need to brush them daily.

Cavalier King Charles Spaniel

This is a really small but sturdy and beautiful dog. Because of their size and friendly and quiet nature, they are great for indoor dogs, as they are moderately active. They are really fond of people and form a strong attachment to them. They are also great for kids because they like to play. Since these dogs are very intelligent, they are easy to train. They have soft personality, so in case they have trouble with doing some trick don't yell at them. This dog has a coat of medium length and sheds particularly in the spring and fall, so that you should brush and comb him regularly.

Labrador Retriever

This is both a working dog and a friendly and loyal companion that lives to serve his family. They are warm and intelligent and because of that they are known as great assistance dogs for the handicapped. Labs are friendly both with people and animals and are eager to please. Because of that, they are easy to train. As he is very energetic, Lab needs to be active in order to be happy. Otherwise, he can use this energy in destructive ways, such as barking and chewing. Labs have a sleek and short double-coat which is easy to take care of. However, they shed a lot so you will need to brush your Lab daily.

Brittany

The Brittany is a very energetic dog that loves to be active all the time, which is a good thing if you spend lots of time outdoors. They are really friendly and thus get on well with children and other pets. He needs at least an hour of everyday exercise and if you don't meet his need for exercise, he will find other ways to let out this energy and you may not like his ways of doing that. They are sensitive to harsh treatment. In that sense, it is important to train them gently and use positive reinforcement. They are not heavily coated so that you can brush them once a week.

Papillon

Papillons are a good choice because they are smart, friendly and easy to train. Although they are small in size, they think of themselves as big dogs having great personalities. The owner of a papillon needs to be strong-willed and establish himself as the leader of the pack. They adapt to any living conditions, either an apartment or rural areas. Generally, they are playful and curious and need early socialization. Papillons are energetic and great in obedience training. They need about half an hour of exercise every day. They have long and flowing coat but they don't shed a lot, so that you can brush and comb your papillon once in a week.

Greyhound

These are quiet and clean dogs with a mild and sweet nature. They display a friendly attitude not only towards people but to other dogs as well. They adapt well to apartments and homes with small yards. Since these are independent dogs, they need a confident owner. Although they look like very energetic race dogs, greyhounds are laid-back and mellow and will be satisfied with a casual walk every day. Sometimes, training greyhounds may be challenging because they may be stubborn. They have short coats and don't shed a lot, so that they are easy to maintain.

Puggle

Puggles are cute dogs of fun-loving personality. They are actually a mix between the pug and beagle. Puggles are great with children and since they are sociable, they get on well with other animals. Puggles like to live indoors and they need at least half an hour of exercise every day. They usually bark a lot, and sometimes even howl. Although these dogs are intelligent, they don't always respond to training as you expect them to, as they may be stubborn and are not so eager to please. Although puggles have short coats, they are double-coated, which means that they shed and that you will have to brush them weekly.

Poodle

Poodles are friendly dogs that love children, and since they are really affectionate and protective of their family and home, they are great as family dogs. This breed adapts well to any type of home although they prefer living indoors. They are impressive and highly intelligent dogs, which makes them easy to train but if you don't show authority they tend to take over. When it comes to grooming, their coat needs more time and care to stay healthy and beautiful. You can take your poodle to a professional groomer once in 3 to 6 weeks. They don't shed, so that this breed is a good choice for people with allergies.

Pug

Pugs are funny, friendly and very loyal dogs. This is a quiet and small breed. Pugs are great companions, and thus follow their owners around, want to sleep in their beds and sit in their laps. When kept indoors, they are not very active but they should be walked regularly. Pugs are known as really intelligent dogs but they can sometimes be willful as well, which in some cases makes training difficult. They get on well with kids, other dogs and animals if they are properly socialized. They shed a lot, especially in summer, because they are double-coated, so that you will need to brush your pug regularly.

Shih Tzu

Shih Tzu is a very playful but very gentle and happy dog that creates strong bonds with his owners. Shih Tzu is bred to be a devoted companion. He is a very adaptable breed, so that he easily gets used to any living conditions. Although he enjoys walking outside, he should be kept indoors. He is not a very active dog, so that short walks every day are enough exercise for him. This breed is difficult to housebreak but you should not allow your puppy to go around the house unsupervised and you should definitely be persisted in your training. Your Shih Tzu should be combed and brushed every day because of his long coat.

Chapter 4: What to Do Before and When Your Puppy Comes

I know you are so excited about bringing your puppy home, but before that you need to do some homework first. You need to prepare your home, yard and family members for this little ball of fur. This is a stressful time for your puppy because he will be away from his mother and siblings for the first time, and thus you need to do some preparations to make this transition easier for him.

Before the Big Day Comes

Before the big day comes and your puppy gets to your lovely home, you need to establish some ground rules. First of all, you need to decide who will take the greatest responsibility for the puppy – who will feed him, walk him, take care of visiting the vet, grooming, etc. Establishing this schedule is important because it will help the puppy to get accustomed to the new environment easily.Secondly, decide on the list of words you will use for specific commands. If you and other family members use different commands for the same thing you want your puppy to do, then you will only confuse him. The next thing is making a shopping list. You will need water and food bowls, food, grooming supplies, chew toys, collar and leash, crate, and name tag.

You should also think about puppy-proofing the area where the puppy will spend most of the time. So, check that some potentially dangerous chemicals are stored out of your puppy's reach, tape loose electrical cords, and remove any things that your puppy can easily damage or break. Make sure that any hanging materials, such as runners or tablecloths, are secured. You can also protect anything that is made of wood because puppies like to chew these things. When it comes to your yard, you should put away plastic toys, tools and garden hoses. Also, make sure to secure the places where your puppy can fall into, and put away all the things you think the puppy can put in his mouth. If there are some areas you don't want your puppy to go to, you should fence off these areas. Check your gates and fences to make sure that your puppy can't go under these or stick his head in here.

At the Breeder

While at the breeder, spend about 15 minutes with your puppy to introduce yourself to him. Also, make sure that you have collected all the necessary paperwork and asked the breeder everything you need to know for the beginning.

When you get your puppy, you should ask the breeder when the puppy was fed and what food he was given. Don't change this feeding schedule immediately because the puppy may have some gastric problems. If you want to change the schedule or switch to a different brand of food, so introduce this change gradually.

Car Ride to the Home

Puppies may feel seek when riding because of all the strange sounds, sights and smells. So, you would probably want to make sure to cover your seats with some paper. As you drive back home, your puppy should be in a carrier or crate at the back seat. Also, keep the car ride relaxed and quiet. If the puppy keeps whining, crying and making noise, you can place him on the floor near your feet, because this area appears to them like a den and they may feel relaxed here.

At Home

Now that you have survived the ride from the breeder to your home, it is time to introduce this new member to the rest of the family.

When you get your puppy home, don't simply take him indoors and let him roam on his own. For your youngster, this is one vast and alien environment and he has no direction where to go. The puppy may seem completely lost because the environment is strange, it smells differently and it may appear to your puppy that there is no way out. The first associations your puppy creates when brought to new home will stick with him and will not wear off.

The first thing to do when you get home is to show the puppy his toilet area. The proper way to introduce your puppy to his new home is to take him to the room where he will spend most of his time and where he can find his food and water. Offer some food and water to the puppy and later on you can show him the rest of the house. If you don't want your puppy to enter some rooms, then don't show him these.

Now is the time to introduce the puppy to your and his family members. Introduce the new family members one at a time, allowing your puppy to come to them first and smell them.

The First Night

Your first night with your new puppy will not be a pleasing experience for both of you. The puppy is for the first time separated from his mother and as a pack animal, the puppy instinctively knows that this is dangerous and he will call his pack to come and find him. So, prepare for listening his whining and crying all night. This is all normal, and your puppy will eventually get used to his new home and new family.

There are some things you can do to make sure your puppy spends the night sleeping instead of crying.

- About seven o'clock, you should take away his food and water; otherwise, your puppy will eliminate in the house or you will need to walk him to the bathroom often.

- Just before you go to bed, play with your puppy for some time in order to tire him enough, so that he will sleep soundly.

- After this, take the puppy to the soiling area and when he goes, praise him.

Where Should Your Puppy Sleep?

Since dogs don't like to be alone, you should place your puppy to sleep in your bedroom if you don't want to listen to his whining all night. One thing you should not do is let your puppy sleep in your bed, because he will want to sleep there even when he grows up. You should also check on your puppy a few times during the night for bathroom breaks.

How to Stop Your Puppy Crying at Night

When your puppy starts crying, you need to decide if he wants your attention or he needs to relieve himself. When your puppy wants to relive himself, he will typically be quiet for some time and then suddenly start crying. On the other hand, if he cries for some time and you are sure it is not for relieving himself, then you should pat him to soothe him but don't do this too often because the puppy may connect this to good behavior and cry even more. In the morning, carry your puppy to his soiling area and praise him. You should not let him walk because he may go before he gets to the soiling area.

How to Name Your Puppy

Giving your puppy a name can be a difficult task. Dogs don't think of their names as something special; your puppy will simply recognize his name as a particular string of sounds which means that he needs to listen to you carefully. When thinking about coming up with a perfect name for your puppy, you can consider the following suggestions:

- Keep the name simple – avoid long and complicated names because your puppy may not understand it. So, it is best to keep the name short and simple, up to three syllables long. Some good choices are also names which are not only short but end in a vowel, because they have a distinctive sound and are easy to pronounce.

- Don't use names that sound like commands – try to avoid names which in any way resemble some basic commands, such as sit, come or shake, because the dog may later on confuse these with his name.

To establish a bond between the puppy and his name, you should always cheerfully tell his name whenever he looks at you and focuses his attention on you.

***

The first few days will give you an opportunity to establish yourself as the leader of the pack. You need to spend lots of time with your puppy so as to establish some foundation for good habits. It is essential to praise your puppy for good and never punish him for bad behavior.

Chapter 5: What Kind of Behavior to Expect from Your Puppy

Although we mostly enjoy our puppies being puppies, their behavior may sometimes be frustrating or even worrying. In some cases, you can't do anything except let your puppy be what he is. However, there are certain situations when you need to react and correct his behavior in a way he will understand.

Now, you may wonder who wouldn't love these little puffy cutes following you everywhere or waging their tails when they see you. Well, very soon you will find out that these are not the only things your cute youngster does. Some annoying things that you will have to deal with include acting aggressively, crying all night, peeing indoors, chewing, nipping, biting and barking. Even though these belong to that normal puppy behavior, you have to admit that these are not so cute. There are also things which should worry you a bit, such as upset tummy, endless hiccups and breathing erratically, in which case you should visit your vet.

How Does the Normal Puppy Behavior Look Like?

Well, there are certain things that puppies do and which are perfectly normal in their canine family, but now when they are in their new home, such a behavior should be discouraged. For instance, puppies commonly tend to chew, growl and whine when left alone. Also, bear in mind that the way your puppy behaves in the first couple of days in your home may be quite different from his behavior later on. This is simply because he needs some time to get used to this new environment, new members of his pack, new smells and new sights. In the beginning, you puppy may cling to you, because as a pack animal, he knows it is important to stay in the pack to survive. Some puppies may also feel anxious or scared and sleep more.

The first thing you need to understand is that your puppy behaves according to its instincts and its basic needs, which include food, water, sleep, elimination and attention. They learn quickly, waiting for you to show them what to do and what they shouldn't do. Puppies learn best when you set up a routine and stick to it because they are creatures of habit. So, if you use one method to change his bad behavior, stick to it; otherwise, you'll only confuse your puppy.

Another thing to have in mind is that puppies, just like kids, have short attention spans. In other words, you will need to spend lots of time to teach them something. Once you notice that he has made some slight progress, don't think that you can stop now. If you do that, he will slide backwards. So, you need to practice this every day until it becomes his new habit.

Here you can find a list of common puppy behavior:

- Excessive barking

Your puppy can't talk, so it's normal for him to bark. Most of the time, your puppy will bark to attract your attention. Unfortunately, you will need some time to figure out what your youngster actually wants to tell you –he is hungry, thirsty, wants to go outside, he is bored, etc. So, barking is normal but excessive barking is not. For instance, your puppy may bark or whine when you left him home alone. If you ignore this and let him stay alone, then he will soon enough learn that he can survive on his own until you come back. On the other hand, some puppies may be really hysterical when left alone and don't show any improvement in overcoming this. In this case, you may get some signs of separation anxiety, so that you will need some help with overcoming this problem. Whenever your puppy starts barking, you should try to find out the reason behind it, particularly when it is excessive barking in question, which you should always discourage.

- Biting and nipping

You may be surprised how often your puppy uses his teeth to bite. However, it is not surprising at all because when in a litter, this is the only way young puppies use to communicate with one another. Although there are some breeds that tend to bite, nip or mouth more than others, all puppies enjoy doing this. When your puppy bites, you shouldn't think that he does this because he is aggressive or wants to hurt you. He is simply following his instincts. For some people, this may be quite cute but this kind of behavior should be discouraged. Imagine this – it's cute when your puppy nips at your hand but imagine your puppy as an adult dog doing this. All of a sudden it may stop being so cute, right?

- Chewing

All puppies love to chew although some breeds (such as terriers, retrievers, herding breeds) chew with a greater persistence and intensity than others. Even though your puppy doesn't know why he does this, he still does it. You will notice this particularly during the period when your puppy's teeth start developing so that your puppy will need to chew everything. This chewing helps your puppy to relive the stress he feels (yes, puppies can be stressed out as well), strengthen the jaw, as well as to prevent plaque and tartar from building up on his teeth. Since chewing is important for your puppy and to his health, you should just teach him what he is allowed to chew and what he is not.

- Guarding

Another normal puppy behavior is guarding his toys, food or treats. When you come to think about it, puppies live with many siblings and they have to fight with them to keep their food, toys or other stuff. However, this kind of behavior can sometimes be dangerous, and thus it is important to address this issue while your puppy is still young. This desire to guard comes naturally and is particularly pronounced in some breeds, such as German shepherds and Rottweilers.

- The puppy crazies

This refers to that hyper behavior which most puppies show somewhere between 4pm and 8pm. Your puppy tends to behave like this because he gets easily over-stimulated and over-tired. When you take into account that his nervous system is not yet mature and doesn't know what to do with this, then it's not surprising why your puppy behaves in this manner. Some puppies may simply run around and bark a little and then need to take a rest. On the other hand, your puppy may be one of those who are so over-excited that they jump on your furniture, nip everything they can, bark and yelp. When this happens you need to do something to change this kind of behavior. For instance, sometimes it may be enough just to firmly say "no" while at other times you will need to redirect his energy to some other, quieter games. In case these two tricks don't help, you can give your puppy some time to go on with his crazies in a separate room or in his crate.

Chapter 6: Toilet Training

Every puppy is different and thus you will be faced with different challenges. But if you now start worrying because it appears that your puppy simply doesn't get the house training the way you have hoped, don't be desperate because there are certain things that may facilitate this process.

- Think of your puppy as of a baby. This youngster still hasn't developed the ability to control his bladder and bowels while at the same time, he seems to eat more and thus eliminate more.

- When your puppy develops this "den" instinct, he will also develop the bowel and bladder control in order not to soil the den, i.e. is your house.

- Don't get desperate because most puppies are completely housetrained when they are about 6 months old. During this period you will notice some progress but also get discouraged by frequent mistakes. You just need to stick to the rules and wait for your puppy to get the hang of it.

Here are the rules you should stick to if you want to house train your puppy:

- Let your puppy go frequently to his soiling area so as to prevent him soiling your house.

- When your puppy eliminates in the soiling area, always reward and praise him.

- Even when your puppy makes some mistake and eliminates in the house, never punish him because this may have negative consequences.

- Set a regular feeding schedule. Some puppies eliminate immediately after a meal while some others eliminate after half an hour or an hour. You shouldn't free feed your puppy, because this may disrupt this feeding schedule, but also your puppy won't associate you as the leader of the pack.

- Know when your puppy last eliminated so that you can approximately expect the next elimination. You should also know that puppies need to eliminate about every half an hour, but luckily, puppies sleep a lot. This of course varies from one breed to another, but you can observe and try to figure out your puppy's schedule.

How to Toilet Train Your Puppy

Method 1

The best way to train your puppy is to keep him into a small area with a crate. In this way, you will encourage the development of this den instinct in your puppy, so that the puppy will learn where he should and where he shouldn't eliminate. In other words, you will confine the puppy to this den-like area and then you will diligently provide him with an access outside the den where the puppy can eliminate. Just follow the steps bellow to learn how to perform this exercise.

First you need to choose some toilet area, which should be quickly accessible to your puppy. In case you live in an apartment, you can use a pen or your bathroom. But if you live in a house, it will be easier to use some outside area. If this is the case, this will be the primary toilet area but you will use an indoor pen for training.

Prepare your home for the training and get the necessary items. You will need paper towels and something to remove urine stains and odor. You will also need a crate for your puppy and a pen that you will use for exercise. Put this exercise pen in the room where you spend most time. It is also advisable to first place some tarp on the floor and then place the pen on it to prevent the puppy from dirtying your carpet. Some rewards used for housetraining can also be helpful, so keep these near the toilet area.

Method 2

First, keep your puppy confined in his pen and paper the floor. Also, place his food and water bowls here as well as his toys. At first, you will notice how your puppy makes a real mess with the papers, he may chew them, eliminate on them and this is all normal. What you have to do is just remove the papers and replace them with some fresh ones. Later on, you will notice how your puppy has one preferred spot where he eliminates. When you notice this, you can start removing some of the papers, starting with those which are the farthest from his chosen spot. Remove the papers gradually, until you need to keep just one piece of paper on the floor. You can then place the paper where you want and the puppy will eliminate there. Don't get discouraged if it appears that your puppy has made some progress and then reverts back and you again need to paper the whole floor. If you stick to this technique, you will manage to paper train your puppy.

Taxi Service

This actually means that you take up the puppy in your arms and take him to the toilet area. In this way, you will prevent the mistakes, i.e. prevent your puppy from eliminating somewhere on the way to the toilet area. When you get the puppy to the toilet area, let him eliminate and praise him afterwards. You should do this immediately after your puppy wakes up, no matter whether this is in the morning or any other part of the day. You should also provide your puppy with this taxi service after meals, drinking water a lot, after playing and whenever you think your puppy should go.

You should apply this tactic for about a month or until your puppy is about 3 months old, which is a period at which your puppy should have at least some kind of control over his bladder and bowels. If you try to observe some warnings, you may get disappointed. When your puppy is about to potty, you will not get any warning but when your puppy starts circling or sniffing, you may get the idea what your puppy is about to do. Until your puppy gains more control over his bladder and bowels, you shouldn't let him go around freely outside his pen or den. Another important factor in house training is rewarding and praising your puppy for good behavior. In this way, you will speed up this training process a bit. Don't rush your puppy and never punish him for mistakes, and always bear in mind that puppies are completely trained when they are about 6 months old or even older.

Chapter 7: Obedience Training

Obedience training is an important thing to do, as it can be rewarding both for your dog and for you. If you think that puppies can't or shouldn't be trained, you are so wrong. As you can notice by yourself, your puppy's behavior is always changing and if you leave some issues unresolved, they may get even worse as your puppy gets older. So, the perfect time for beginning with obedience training is now.

Although you can't expect this kind of training to address all kinds of problems you have with your puppy, it creates a kind of communication between you and him, and in that way it forms the basis for dealing with various issues. Another important aspect of obedience training is the idea that is helps you teach your dog the hierarchy in your pack. In other words, when your dog learns the commands you have tried to teach him, he also shows his respect for you and recognizes his subordinate position in the pack.

Dogs generally need proper training in order to forget about some of their canine habits and behave appropriately in our world. Your puppy may destroy some of your belongings, soil your house, or bark all night and these are all perfectly normal things for him. However, effective communication helps you to teach your dog how to use this energy to do something that is recognized as more acceptable.

When beginning with this kind of training, you should bear in mind that this should be fun both for your dog and for you. If you manage to train your dog well, you will also boost his self-confidence, so that consequently you can allow him more freedom. Also, begin this training with the things your puppy already knows or things that are a bit familiar to him. Once your dog has mastered a few commands, you can try to make these more advanced and challenging by changing the training location and introducing distractions. These training sessions should be short because dogs have short attention spans, and if you notice that your dog is looking somewhere around you and avoid making an eye contact with you, then you should know that he is actually telling you that he is tired and he needs a break.

A very important element of obedience training is rewarding and praising your dog for good behavior. You should never forget to praise your dog and give him some treat. In this way, the dog will make a connection between the reward and a certain kind of behavior. If you reward him often, he will learn faster and that's how this training works. On the other hand, you should avoid reprimanding your dog. Even when you do this, make sure that your reprimands are short and immediate; otherwise, the dog won't understand the meaning of your scolding. Also, if you use reprimands a lot, they will lose any meaning and the dog will simply ignore them. On the contrary, if you praise and reward your dog often and use reprimands rarely, they will have a stronger effect and the dog will know that he has done something wrong.

Come

Description: Your puppy comes to you when commanded.

Step 1: Choose the command you want to use for this trick. For instance, it can be *Here* or *Come*.

Step 2: Stand close to your puppy and say the command.

Step 3: When the puppy comes close to you, praise and reward him.

Step 4: Now, go a bit further away from your puppy and say the command again.

Step 5: Reward you puppy with lots of praise.

Step 6: Use this command throughout a day when you are near your puppy.

Walk with Me

Description: Your puppy learns to walk by your side.

Step 1: Attach a leash to your puppy and have him walk by your side. If he pulls you away, go in the opposite direction.

Step 2: Whenever your puppy walks close to you, reward him with lots of praise and a treat.

Step 3: You can gradually introduce the command *Walk with Me* or *With Me*. After every few steps your puppy makes walking near you without pulling, give him a treat.

Step 4: Practice this for about 5 minutes, several times a day.

Sit

Description: This will teach your puppy to sit on command.

Step 1: Carefully observe your puppy's behavior and when he sits, praise him and give him a treat.

Step 2: Repeat this as long as it is needed for your puppy to make a connection between sitting down and a reward.

Step 3: You can gradually introduce the command *Sit*. Whenever your puppy sits down, say the command, praise the puppy and give him a treat.

Step 4: Keep these training sessions short and always praise your puppy when he obeys the command.

Stay

Description: Your puppy stays at one place until you release him.

Step 1: Command your puppy to sit and give him a treat if he acts accordingly.

Step 2: Say the command *Stay*, go a step or two away from your puppy, wait for a few seconds and call him to come to you.

Step 3: Praise your puppy and always give him a treat when he performs well.

Step 4: Repeat the same procedure several times. Later on, you can prolong the time your puppy stays at one spot.

Leave it!

Description: Your puppy leaves an item when commanded to do so.

Step 1: First, have your puppy on his leash and drop a few treats in front of him.

Step 2: Pull him back when he starts for the treats, say his name followed by the command *Leave it*.

Step 3: Give him a treat when he looks at you and then praise him.

Step 4: You can repeat this training session several times but keep them short.

Chapter 8: Proper Ways to Walk Your Puppy

When you get your little puppy, you definitely feel so eager to take him out and show him off around your neighborhood. Most people think that it's enough to take a collar and leash and your little one will exactly know what he has to do. Well, it's not always that easy.

The first thing you should keep in mind is the right time for your puppy to get him out into that great unknown world out there. It is recommended to keep your puppy inside and avoid dog parks until he has all of his core vaccinations. Luckily, you can train your puppy even before you walk him out. Normally, a puppy can be walked out between 3 and 6 months old, which is also a good period to begin with some obedience training. Here are some of the steps you should follow to walk your puppy properly:

- **Introduce your dog to a collar and leash**

You can do this while your puppy is really young, like a few weeks old. Try to slip on the collar and leash while he is doing something positive like eating or playing. In this way, the puppy will connect the collar and leash to something positive and wont fight it later on.

- **Go for a walk**

If your puppy still can't go out and meet other dogs, you can give him a tour around your apartment, house or your backyard. Attach his leash and slowly walk him around, so that the puppy can get used to you leading him. Naturally, puppies form a strong connection to the one they look at as their pack leader and they will follow you anywhere. Now, you just need to give him some time to get used to the leash.

- **Help him learn to follow**

The point of using a leash is to lead your dog, not let him lead you. As this can often be the case with larger breeds, it is important to learn your puppy to follow you; otherwise, it may be too late to teach him this when he grows up.

If you notice that your puppy pulls you, then walk in the opposite direction. You will have to do this a lot in the beginning, but eventually the puppy will get used to following you. You can also praise your puppy and give him some reward for showing his good manners.

Chapter 9: Play Time

When you look at two puppies playing, you'll see that they are not gentle at all. But if you have some doubts about whether your puppy is aggressive or just playful, look at some of the observations below:

- When a puppy wants to play, he will raise his rear and lower his front end and head. Also, he will most certainly wag his tail, dash back and forth and make yipping noises.

- You'll recognize that your puppy is being aggressive by his gaze and stance. He will fix his gaze, stand still and growl in a threatening manner. You should also know that dogs are generally not being aggressive all of a sudden. Instead, they react in such a way because they feel threatened or they receive some confusing stimulus.

What to Do When Your Puppy is Aggressive?

If your puppy is being aggressive, you should consult with your vet so as to try to determine some possible causes of this kind of behavior. If it appears that your puppy is sometimes too aggressive when he plays, you can use some of these tricks to curb this inappropriate play.

- If the pup is aggressive when playing with you, and if, for instance, he hurts you with his claws or teeth, you should stop playing and say something like *Ouch*, so that the puppy knows you disapprove of this kind of play.

- You can also use a spray of water to distract his behavior. However, don't do something that will scare your puppy.

- If your puppy is aggressive when playing with some specific toy, simply replace it with another one.

- If all of this doesn't help, take your puppy to his crate and leave him to settle down. You can give him a toy to play with and keep him occupied.

- In any case, you shouldn't act aggressively when you try to manage your puppy's aggressive behavior. Also, never grab his muzzle, shake him, hit him or do anything that can hurt your puppy. This kind of behavior can only make the situation worse and the puppy may behave even more aggressively.

Why Is Playing Important?

Playing is essential for you puppy's mental, physical and emotional development. If your puppy doesn't get enough exercise where he will be allowed to express his natural behavior, he may start showing some signs of a variety of behavior problems, such as destroying your belongings or doing some attention-seeking activities.

Playing with your puppy will first of all, keep him busy and tire him enough to keep him quiet later during the night. Also, plays and exercises channel his energy into constructive and fun activities. On another level, playing with your puppy will deepen your relationship and make the bond between you two stronger.

Tips on Playing with Your Puppy

- When you play with your puppy, it's not advisable to play on the floor. When you are down on his level, he can get overexcited and then scratch you or pounce on you.

- Also, don't imitate your puppy's behavior when playing with him. In this way, he will perceive this as if playing with another puppy or dog and you know that dogs play rough, so, bear in mind that he can unintentionally hurt you. It's always better to stay in a leadership role when you play with your pup.

- Since dogs love routine, you can choose some time a day for playing with your puppy.

- You should not let your puppy play for too long because they also need sleep for proper maturation and development.

- Another thing to bear in mind while playing with your puppy is to make a few breaks, which serves to prevent your puppy from getting overexcited and to draw his attention back to you. Also, don't play with your puppy to the point when he gets bored.

What Are the Games that Puppies Love?

A nice activity for your youngster is a stroll. This is a nice opportunity for him to jump, run and explore. These walks should be short (5 minutes for each month of your puppy's age is enough). Also, you give him a great opportunity for exploration, experiencing new smells, sights, seeing other animals and people. So, although a stroll is primarily a physical exercise, it is intellectually stimulating as well.

The next fun game you can play with your puppy is hide and seek. You will need a help of a friend who will need to hold you puppy until you hide somewhere. Then you should call your puppy's name every few seconds until he finds you.

Fetch is another game that can be played with your puppy. You can play it outside in your backyard or even in your living room. It will help your little friend follow instructions and improve his focus. It is pretty simple to play. You first need to pique his interest, and then toss a toy and instruct him to retrieve it. Although most puppies get the hang of this in no time, you can first show your puppy what you expect him to do. Don't get your puppy overtired, but play for 10 minutes and then take a break. Use soft toys that your puppy can easily hold in his mouth, and avoid wooden sticks.

If you like swimming, you can bring your puppy with you. You can first get him swim in a small pool before you take him to a lake, for instance. Most puppies like water and this is a great activity because it won't put stress on their joints. You can also bring some of his toys, preferable the ones which can float, and let him chase them. Since your puppy will quickly become tired, keep this game short (about 10 minutes is enough). It should be noted that if your puppy appears to be afraid of water, don't force him to enter the pool.

Chapter 10: How to Socialize Your Puppy

Sometimes you may notice that your puppy is shy, he hides when some of your friends come or growls at people who try to get close to him. When your little puppy snaps at some passengers while you take him for a walk, then you should start worrying about this kind of behavior. In that sense, socialization is important if you want a well-behaved and healthy dog.

What Is Puppy Socialization?

There is a period in a puppy's live, known as the "sensitive period", when puppies should learn what the things are like in the world out there. During this period they accept everything they have pleasant experience with but, on the other hand, they are not immune to fears, pain and trauma. This is an important period because they learn about a variety of sights, smells, sounds, as well as numerous experiences important for their development. Another important aspect of early socialization is that when a puppy learns that there are so many pleasant experiences around, he won't be afraid of new experiences and will be confident to deal with them once he is faced with novel situations.

Many experts say that if socialization doesn't come early, it can be too late when this "sensitive period" is over. It is usually best to start socializing your puppy when he is somewhere between 12 and 16 weeks old. If you miss the opportunity to begin with socialization on time, your puppy may grow up into a skittish and shy dog.

The Importance of Socialization

Why socialization is so important can be seen by observing the behavior of undersocialized dogs. They are not flexible, meaning that they don't respond to new situations adequately. Instead, they approach anything new with fear and don't like any changes, which may make them aggressive and fearful. Also, some undersocialized dogs don't like to go outside, or they feel so much afraid that they pull you away back home, so that it is impossible to walk them. Some dogs walk with their tails down, which shows that they are afraid and that they don't feel safe. Sometimes, you can also see dogs barking at everything and everyone. So, if you socialize your puppy, you will avoid a variety of behavior problems.

How to Socialize Your Puppy

Now, you are probably wondering how to do this socialization thing. It is pretty simple. You just need to take your puppy almost everywhere you go – to the mall, parks, pet shops, bus stations, to the beach, etc. You can take him in your arms, by car or walk him. When you walk him, don't be afraid to encourage him to smell some flowers, scramble among rocks or even dig if he feels like digging. Also, teach your puppy to use stairs or even carry him in your arms while in an elevator. You should provide him with an opportunity to experience many surfaces as well.

Another part of socialization is to introduce your puppy to all kinds of people. There are cases of people feeling embarrassed of their dogs barking at people of different race. So, you can always carry some treats when you walk your puppy and then encourage your neighbors, passers-by and children to pat your puppy and then you should praise him and give him one of the treats. All these different people will provide your puppy with extraordinary experiences, and thus he will not be afraid of strangers when he grows up.

What you have just read can be applied to animals as well. If possible, you should let your puppy get familiar with different animals. However, take good care of your puppy when he is near other adult dogs, especially those dogs you don't know. Since you don't know how these dogs may react to your puppy, you should avoid them at first until you know for sure that they are healthy and well-mannered.

Since it is not unusual for dogs to be afraid of sounds unfamiliar to them, you should spend some time working on this area of socialization as well. There are all sorts of sounds that may be a possible cause of phobia if your puppy is not introduced to them in his early days. These may be police sirens, birdsong, ringtones, doorbells, banging pots, music, etc. As with everything else, when your little pup once gets familiar with all the possible sounds that he can hear in his environment, he will be more likely to positively react to some novel sounds.

What to Do if Your Puppy Is Shy

In case you see that your puppy shies away when you want to introduce him to your friend, you should not force him to come close. Let him stay in his comfort zone and allow him to explore at his own pace. After a while, you may notice that he comes closer until he relaxes completely near this person. It is also important to instruct this person to pay no attention to the puppy as he goes near, because he may get scared and retreat back. If you really want to help your puppy overcome this shyness, you will also avoid using food to lure him to come. As you see your youngster approaching and exploring, you should praise him softly and encouragingly. However, if your puppy doesn't feel like meeting this person, don't push him but postpone the meeting for some other time.

Chapter 11: Introducing Your Puppy to Other Pets

If you already have pets, you should know that they won't share your enthusiasm about bringing a new puppy home. For some reason, other pets tend to perceive these cute puppies as annoying, and they particularly won't like all that attention you give to this new member of your family. Thus, you will need to give all of you some time to get used to one another.

What Can You Do to Ease the Tension?

When they get a new puppy, people usually give all their attention to him, forgetting about their resident pets. However, this is not a proper approach. It is important to give all preference to the resident pets, and this is especially important in the beginning. You won't hurt your little one's feelings. This will only teach him to respect the resident pets and he will act accordingly. In that sense, you should always feed your resident pets first and if you feed your puppy three times a day, divide your other pets' meals into three parts as well. Always play, greet and treat your resident pets first. Also, in case your resident pet approaches you during your play with the puppy, don't neglect him but focus your attention on him; otherwise, you'll let your puppy push the other pets aside.

How to Introduce Your Puppy to Other Dogs

Since your older dog won't be so much happy about sharing his space with a new member of the family, you should introduce them in some neutral area or at least bring your older dog outside to meet the puppy. No matter how your dog reacts, focus on your dog and stay calm. It is best to introduce them at a time you know your dog is calm and relaxed. You will need someone's help with this. Have someone handling your puppy while you slowly approach with your dog on a leash. Give some treats to your dog and when it seems that he accepts the puppy, tell your friend to bring the puppy into your home. Leave the dogs, paying attention all the time on their interaction. If the puppy gets afraid and comes to you, encourage him but let the dogs work that out on their own.

How to Introduce Your Puppy to Cats

Cats are typically not fond of living together with puppies. So, don't have high expectations when you bring your puppy home. Your cat will probably wait for the puppy to approach enough so that he can then bat him on the nose. Since cats defend their space, you can expect your cat to bat or growl at your puppy often, particularly in the beginning. Don't try to correct his behavior because it will only make it worse. In the beginning, you can place the puppy in a crate and allow your cat to walk around the room on his own. If the puppy starts getting mad, try to calm him down. When you notice that your cat is calm and nonchalant when close to the puppy, you can try to bring the two together. Have some toy at hand to divert your puppy's attention if he starts acting up.

How to Introduce Your Puppy to Caged Pets

If your pet is caged, you should bring your puppy near the cage after a meal and during playtime. Bring some of the puppy's toys as well, sit near the cage and pet the puppy. You should repeat this often to allow the resident pet to become familiar with the puppy. Repeat this exercise frequently throughout the day.

Chapter 12: Grooming

If you want a healthy and happy puppy, you need to establish good grooming habits. Since this may require some time and lots of effort, especially in the beginning, it is better to set some schedule and stick to it. This will make the whole grooming experience more pleasant and easier to go through both for you and your dog. However, this will not come all by itself.

First, you will need to somehow teach your puppy to associate grooming with things that he likes. How exactly to do this? As with obedience training, you will need to use some tricks and make your puppy at least tolerate grooming if not enjoy it. To achieve this, you will need to show your puppy that trimming his nails, cleaning his ears or bathing and brushing are followed by some great things, such as some new toys or special treats. So, for instance, you should brush your puppy for a few seconds and then give him a treat, continue brushing and give him another treat, so that eventually this will be a pleasant and not frightening experience for your little one.

The second key thing to successful grooming is to take it easy and slow. This may be a tough one especially if your puppy doesn't like to be inspected or regularly cleaned. If you want to teach your puppy to tolerate the time spent this way, you don't want to frighten him. First of all, it is important to be relaxed, because when you are calm, your puppy will be relaxed, too. So, pay attention to your body language and speak in a soothing and calm voice. Also, if you all of a sudden take your puppy and throw it into a bathtub, you may be sure that this attempt will end in a complete disaster. Instead, take some time to introduce your puppy to bathing, clipping nails and brushing. So, you may for instance, clip one of his nails, and then give him a treat. The next day, clip another nail and give him a treat. The thing is that when you want to do everything in one go, your puppy will be frightened of all those new things and when you break these tasks into parts and give your puppy some time to get familiar with every part and see that there's nothing to be afraid of, he will accept grooming without making any fuss.

How to Start

Since puppies are more sensitive than adult dogs, you can first start by touching his paws, examining his mouth and ears, restraining him in your arms and after this you should give him a treat. In this way, you will form a good base for an effortless grooming experience. If, for instance, your puppy struggles to break free and get away from you when you restrain him, don't let him go but hold him tight. Once he relaxes, let him go and give him a reward. The idea here is to show your puppy that struggling won't give him freedom. Instead, he will learn that what he has to do is to tolerate restraint.

A General Health Check

It won't take you much time and it is important to give your puppy a general
once-over every day. You will become familiar with his body, so that you
will easily detect any changes that you may want your vet to check. But also,
it will help you and your puppy establish grooming as a habit.

What Does Grooming Include?

Grooming your puppy includes bathing him, brushing, keeping his eyes and ears clean, trimming his nails and brushing his teeth.

Bathing

Since some dogs don't need to be bathed that often, and some breeds even shouldn't (some breeds tend to develop some skin irritations if bathed too often), you should speak to your vet or groomer to see how often to bathe your puppy.

As dogs are not that crazy about bathing, you should use some tricks when it comes to bathing time. To associate this with some pleasant experience, you should spend a couple of days walking your puppy to the bathroom area. Then, you should spend several days just getting your puppy to spend a few minutes in a tub. You should also give him some treats and his favorite toys to play with.

Brushing

How often you will need to brush your puppy depends on his breed, more precisely on his type of coat. There are different brushes to choose from and before doing this, it is a wise decision to speak with a groomer or a vet first. Some breeds naturally like brushing while some others find it uncomfortable. In any case, you should give your puppy some treats after brushing.

If your puppy doesn't like brushing, you should slowly introduce it into his grooming routine. First of all, you should brush him lightly and gently and start with the areas your puppy seems to be the least sensitive about. After a few strokes, give him some treat. Gradually, you can prolong this brushing time.

Nail Trimming

If your dog's nails are not trimmed when needed, they may get too long, which may cause infection and pain. In some cases, a dog's toes can twist, which leads to skeletal damage. When it comes to the clippers to use, there are two types – a scissors type and a guillotine type. You can go to a pet store and see which ones you feel more comfortable working with.

To get your puppy used to trimming his nails, you should first spend a few days just touching his paws, so that he gets used to his paws being handled. After this give him a treat. Spend the following few days on another step and that is holding your puppy's paw and touching the clippers to one of his nails. Don't trim the nail, just touch it and give your puppy a treat immediately. Now, when your dog gets used to this, you can trim a nail or two and give him a treat. When trimming your dog's nails, besides clippers, you should also have some clotting powder, so that you can use it if you accidentally cut the quick.

Another thing to pay a very close attention to is where to trim. It is easier if your puppy has clear nails, so that you can easily see the pink quick. You should cut about two or three millimeters from the quick. Don't cut closer than that. If your dog has dark nails, you should cut one little sliver of nail at a time. After every cut, look at the exposed edge of the nail and when you see a pink or gray oval, you should stop trimming. And don't forget his dewclaws.

Eyes and Ears

To clean your puppy's eyes, you can use a soft and damp cloth. In case you notice some yellow or green discharge, inflammation or redness, you should visit your vet.

The same amount of care goes for the ears as well. If you notice some unusual smell, waxy buildup or inflamed skin, speak to your veterinarian about this. You should also consult your vet about the cleaners and technique used for cleaning your puppy's ears.

Brushing Your Puppy's Teeth

Brushing your puppy's teeth may seem as unnecessary in the beginning, but this will do him good later on in his life. To brush his teeth, you can use a toothbrush and toothpaste specially made for dogs. If your dog doesn't like this, you may use a piece of gauze instead, wrap it around your finger and use this to clean his teeth. You should clean his teeth two to three times a week. Another way to keep his teeth healthy is to give him a lot of things to chew.

This will also help in strengthening his jaw and relieving stress.

Parasite Prevention

Protecting your puppy from different parasites is important both for you and him. You should protect him from fleas, ticks, heartworms and intestinal worms. Some of the diseases these parasites may cause include skin infections, anemia, and Lyme disease, and when it comes to heartworms and intestinal worms, they can even kill a dog. You should know that these parasites and diseases are contagious to humans as well. Hopefully, you can always speak to your veterinarian and find the right preventatives to protect both your puppy and yourself.

How to Choose a Groomer

If you want to hire a professional groomer, you can ask for recommendations from your vet, friends, dog trainers, animal shelters, pet stores, etc. However, before you take your dog to a groomer, you should make sure that this is a reputable place. So, before taking your dog there, visit the place alone and do a little investigation. Take a look around the place to see if it looks clean, to check whether it is too loud, cold or unpleasant, if the staff is knowledgeable and friendly, and if they handle dogs you can see gently. Also, check the place where the animals are kept before and after grooming. A reputable groomer will also allow you to watch a grooming session and will always ask you for your dog's vaccine records.

Chapter 13: Feeding Time

Puppies grow and develop really quickly, and thus puppy food should provide all their nutritional needs. A well-balanced food will give your puppy all the protein, minerals and vitamins needed for building a strong and healthy body. Since there are so many types and brands of dog food, it is really hard to choose the one for your puppy. Hopefully, you can use a few guidelines when making a choice.

It is recommended to use puppy food until your puppy is a year old. In some cases, but this is really rare, some puppies should stop eating this food because they may be developing too quickly. In such cases, it is better to consult with your veterinarian, since such a rapid growth may sometimes cause panosteitis or long bone disease.

Types of Puppy Food

There are three different types of food and these are moist, semi moist and dry kibble. Of these three, the best option is dry kibble because this type of food contains the greatest amount of meat protein. Other things worth mentioning are that it is easier to digest, it is cost-effective, more practical and better for keeping a puppy's teeth clean. If you use dry kibble, you can mix it with some warm water or canned meat.

Moist puppy food is expensive and if not stored properly, it spoils quickly. It is mostly composed of water, which means that it contains fewer nutrients. Also, it is not really good for teeth, because it stays on the surface of the teeth more easily, so that in the long run the puppy's teeth will become more prone to cavities. On the plus side, it is easy to digest. It is probably best to use both dry kibble and moist food and combine them. You can vary them from meal to meal or mix them together.

When it comes to semi-moist food, it is practical to use and easy to digest but it doesn't have any dental benefits as dry kibble, and it is usually expensive. It also contains high amounts of sugar, preservatives and salt, and thus is said to lead to hyperactivity and obesity.

If your puppy sometimes refuses to eat his food, never give him the food you eat or the food from your table, because this food will not provide him with all the necessary nutrients he needs. However, you can sometimes give him a little yogurt to improve the work of his digestive system. Also, try to avoid feeding your puppy while you eat, because he will always expect to get some food from the table.

Tips on Feeding Your Puppy

Until your puppy reaches six months of age, you should feed him three times a day. Then, you can reduce this to feeding him once in the morning and once in the evening. Feed your puppy at the same time every day and try to feed him at some quiet area where he will not be disturbed.

The ideal amount of food depends on the breed of your puppy but you can check the package, as it always gives some information on this. Generally speaking, larger breeds and more energetic dogs need more calories than those smaller breeds or relaxed, quiet and laid-back dogs. Also, bear in mind that you should not feed your puppy too much, because you don't want him to be overweight.

When it comes to water, it is true that puppies need lots of water but if you let your puppy have a bowl of water available all the time, you will have some problems with house training, as you will encourage him to drink water even when he is not thirsty, and then you'll have a real problem. So, it's better to give your puppy water at some schedule and take him outside after that to relieve himself. As your puppy develops his bladder control and as he gets older, you can leave a bowl of water for him.

Chapter 14: Vet Visit

When you get your puppy, it is advisable to take him to your vet for a health check. The puppy has probably already got some vaccinations and this is the information you can get from the breeder. Depending on the breed, your puppy's tail may have been docked and his dewclaws removed.

Besides a general health check, your vet will also give you some valuable piece of advice on how to keep your puppy healthy and happy. Since you will need to take your puppy to your veterinarian often, it is of great importance to establish good habits from the very beginning. As your puppy may be nervous or anxious when you take him to the vet for the first time, it is advisable to schedule an appointment early in the morning, when the place is less active and less noisy, as there won't be many people and dogs in the waiting room.

While the veterinarian examines your puppy, make sure that your youngster is relaxed. So, you should keep him calm by praising him softly both during and after the examination. If the puppy starts to fidget or make a fuss, try to distract his attention with a wave of your hand, for instance. If you are overly sympathetic in this case, you can make it only worse, because the puppy may understand this as reinforcing this kind of behavior.

When you take your puppy to his first health check, besides his first set of vaccinations, he will also be weighted and be generally examined to check his teeth and gums, eyes, ears, coat, lungs and heart. Your veterinarian may also ask you to bring a stool sample to be tested for parasites.

Also, it is recommended to bring with you any health records you got from the breeder. This will be helpful for your veterinarian, because he will be given a sense of the puppy's previous care. When your veterinarian gives you some recommendations and suggestions for the future health care of your puppy, make sure that you are clear on any of these. Don't be ashamed to ask for clarifications, and if needed, even write these down. Also, feel free to ask anything that you don't know or have doubts about, no matter how trivial it may sound. This will form a good base for taking a good care of your puppy.